# Notes for Grown-Ups & Teachers

Thank you for picking up this book which is for children, young peo[ple...] better understand what LGBT+ means.

This book does not include sex education. This book gives a positive i[mage of gender] and sexual orientation for everyone. Understanding these topics is not only useful for all children and young people, it is potentially life-saving.

We hope you enjoy sharing this book with the children in your class and life. It is designed so that each page can be used as the focus for a lesson, with plenty of opportunities to learn and discuss.

It may be helpful to set some ground rules for class discussions. Make it clear that students can share information about themselves and their own experiences, but that it is entirely up to them. Encourage children to speak in generalities and not about specific people in the class or school. Also, avoid singling children out as representatives for a particular group.

In addition to discussion suggestions, this book includes worksheets and activities. There are accompanying videos at youtube.com/popnolly, and additional classroom resources are available to members at popnolly.com.

**Olly Pike**
Director of Pop'n'Olly Ltd

**Mel Lane & James Canning**
LGBT+ Equality Educators

'Check out the adaptable lesson ideas and worksheets at popnolly.com to explore the topics in this book further.'

First published in 2021
by Pop'n'Olly Ltd

*www.popnolly.com*

Copyright © Olly Pike 2021

All rights reserved. No part of this publication may be reproduced in any material form (including photocopying, in any medium by electronic means or transmission) without the written permission of the copyright owner, except for the use of brief quotations in a book review or scholarly journal.

**ISBN** 978-0-9933407-8-9

# What Does LGBT+ Mean?

## A Guide for Young People (and Grown-Ups)

*Olly Pike,*

*with Mel Lane and James Canning*

Pop'n'Olly

# What's in this Book?

- 6 — Hello!
- 8 — Identity
- 10 — Assigned Sex & Gender
- 11 — Gender as a Spectrum & Pronouns
- 12 — Transgender
- 13 — Non-Binary
- 14 — Intersex (Differences in Sex Development)
- 15 — Gender Stereotypes
- 16 — Romantic Love
- 18 — Sexual Orientation
- 20 — Privilege
- 22 — Discrimination
- 24 — The First Pride
- 26 — How Can I Help?
- 27 — So, What Does LGBT+ Mean?
- 28 — LGBT+ People
- 30 — LGBT+ Flag Guide
- 31 — Need to Talk?
- 32 — Resources
- 35 — Pop'n'Olly
- 36 — Meet the Authors
- 37 — More Classroom Resources
- 38 — Pop'n'Olly Books
- 40 — Thank You

# Hello!

**HELLO** and welcome to this book! My name is Olly. I'm a writer, an illustrator and a YouTuber. I have curly brown hair, I love ice cream and I am a part of the LGBT+ community.

**'But wait...'** I hear you say. **'What does LGBT+ mean?'** Well, that's what this book is about!

You see, being LGBT+ is just one part of me. It's not the only part. But it is a part that I'm proud of and happy to celebrate.

If I wanted to, I could tell you what LGBT+ means in just a few sentences. But sometimes when you get a question answered, it leads to another one and another one and another one!

So, I thought it would be a lot more helpful to explore a whole bunch of different topics with you, all of which will really help you to understand exactly what LGBT+ means.

If I had known what LGBT+ meant when I was growing up, it would have made life a lot easier for me, and I think it would have helped my friends who weren't LGBT+, too!

This book contains a lot of information and lots of ideas which you may or may not have heard before. So take your time reading, there is no rush.

Join me and my balloon friend Pop (he's from my YouTube channel) as we journey through a number of topics together.

There will be lots of things to talk about and do along the way and if you need more help after reading perhaps you can talk to a parent, teacher or grown-up that you trust.

## Olly Pike
Director of Pop'n'Olly Ltd
(He/Him)

# Look Out For...

Throughout this book you may notice different flags. Flags can be a useful way of quickly identifying and representing different groups of people or communities.

Not everyone will use their community's flag or colours, but for some people these flags and colours are important.

On page 30 there is a handy guide to all the different flags and colours you might notice whilst reading.

# Identity

Did you know that you are incredible, one of a kind and that there is no one else on this planet who is exactly like you? Pretty awesome, huh?

But hang on, what exactly is it that makes you... you? Is it your personality? Or is it the way you look? Perhaps it's the way you think? Or what you believe? Maybe it's what you like to do? Or simply where you come from?

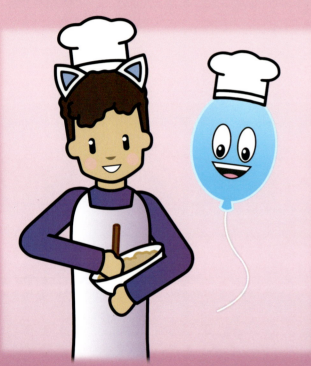

Well, the truth is... all of these things are what make you you! This is called our identity.

You see, our identity is like a recipe.

When baking a cake, lots of different ingredients will be used. The ingredients by themselves do not make the cake, but put them together and you have a masterpiece.

So, just like a cake, our identity is made up of lots of different parts and different parts will make different people, just as different ingredients will make different cakes.

And different is great! After all, the world would be a pretty boring place if we were all exactly the same.

Some parts of our identity might stay the same our whole life, parts like our skin colour or where our family is from. Other parts, like our hobbies, how we like to dress, and even our thoughts and values may change as we grow and learn more about ourselves and the world.

We should all be proud of our identities because it is who we are.

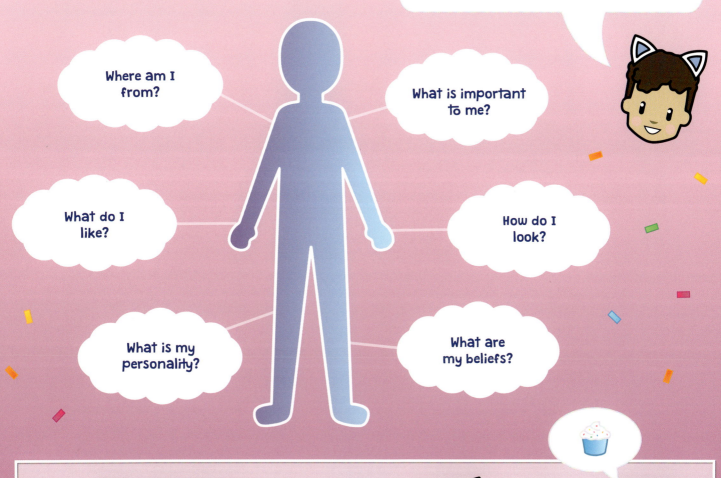

**Try this:** Copy this picture and write in the bubbles all the different parts that make you you. (There is a blank version at the back of this book.)

'In this book we are going to explore more about gender and sexual orientation which are also part of a person's identity.'

- Where am I from?
- What is important to me?
- What do I like?
- How do I look?
- What is my personality?
- What are my beliefs?

## Ask a Friend

Can you share your answers with a friend? See what makes you the same and what makes you different.

The more people you talk to, the more you will see how amazingly diverse our world really is.

# Assigned Sex

When we were born, it's likely a doctor or nurse looked at our body and gave us a label based on what they could see: male or female. This is often called a person's 'assigned sex'.

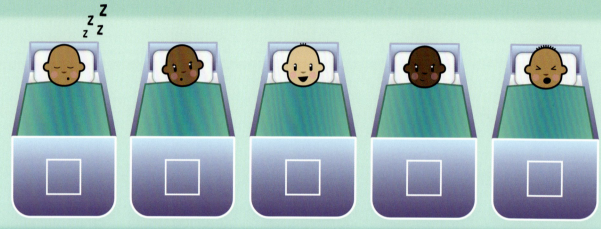

(Some people are born with bodies that are different from what a doctor would consider as a typical male or female body: we will explore this further on page 14.)

# Gender

Gender is different from assigned sex. A person's gender is who they feel that they are, e.g. male, female, both or neither. Gender is usually something a person just knows about themselves, although it can also be something a person discovers about themselves as they grow older.

Most people's gender will be the same as their assigned sex, but this is not always the case for everyone.

When a person's gender is the same as their assigned sex, then this is called 'cisgender'.

# Gender as a Spectrum

Some people find it useful to think of gender as a spectrum - a sliding scale that most people sit on somewhere.

Some people will feel that their place on this spectrum is fixed, whilst others might feel that their position on it can change and move around.

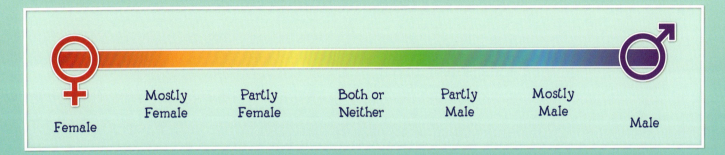

Some people may not see themselves on this spectrum at all. They might see their gender in a completely different way, and they may relate better to a different kind of spectrum or idea about gender altogether.

There are also some cultures around the world who view gender differently, too.

People feel happier and included when their pronouns are respected. There are lots of different types of pronouns, and some of the most commonly used are:

- He, him, his
- She, her, hers
- They, them, theirs

We can't just assume someone's pronouns. If you are not sure about another person's pronouns it is OK to politely ask. Sometimes, a great way to find out someone else's pronouns is to tell them yours first.

If you make a mistake with someone's pronouns, apologise, correct yourself and move on.

# Transgender

Some people feel that their gender does not match their assigned sex.

For example, someone who is assigned male as a baby, but as they grow older, identifies as female.

People who feel this way will often describe themselves as transgender.

A transgender person may feel that their body, or appearance, does not match up with their gender or how they feel about themselves, and they may want to make changes in order to feel more comfortable. Changes such as their name, clothes, pronouns or hairstyle.

However, not all transgender people will make changes, because not all transgender people will have the same experience.

'Every transgender person is unique.'
- Eli Moore, Transgender Artist

# Non-Binary

Some people are non-binary. There are lots of different ways to be non-binary and there are lots of different words used to describe it.

Some non-binary people feel they are a mixture of male and female, some feel they move between the two, and some people feel they are neither male nor female. Some people feel that they don't have a gender at all.

Non-binary will look and feel different for everyone and you can't tell if someone is non-binary just from their appearance. (Some non-binary people may also identify as transgender and some may not.)

'It's important to remember that there is no "one way" to look or be non-binary.'
- Iesha Palmer, UK Charity Worker

# Intersex

## (Differences in Sex Development)

We are all born with sex characteristics. They are the parts of us that a doctor would look at to decide whether our bodies are considered male or female.

Some people are born with sex characteristics that are different (or that develop differently) from what a doctor would consider as typical for an average male or female body.

A person with a body like this may describe themselves as intersex.

Not all intersex people will be the same. The human body can naturally grow and develop in so many different ways, which means there are so many different ways that a person can be intersex.

Some intersex people will identify as female, some will identify as male, some will identify as transgender and/or non-binary, and some will describe themselves as intersex.

Being born with a body like this doesn't mean that there is something wrong with a person, it is just a different way of being human.

'Being born intersex is not a choice and no one should make you feel ashamed of your body or how you identify.'
- Anick Soni, UK-based Intersex Activist

Some people will have sex characteristics that are noticeably different as soon as they are born. Other people may not discover differences in their sex characteristics until they are older.

# Gender Stereotypes

Stereotyping is expecting someone to look, sound or behave in a certain way based on one piece of information about them. It is a bit like trying to guess someone's whole identity based on just one part.

Sometimes we are led to believe that certain clothes, toys, hobbies, jobs, colours and even emotions 'belong' to a particular gender. This is called gender stereotyping. It can make people feel that they should dress, act or behave in a particular way just because of their gender.

For example, someone might not wear a particular piece of clothing, or play with a certain toy, because they think it doesn't match their gender.

Sometimes a person might not pursue a hobby, interest or even a career because they feel they are 'not the right gender' for it.

All of this can make life feel very restricted and full of 'gender rules'.

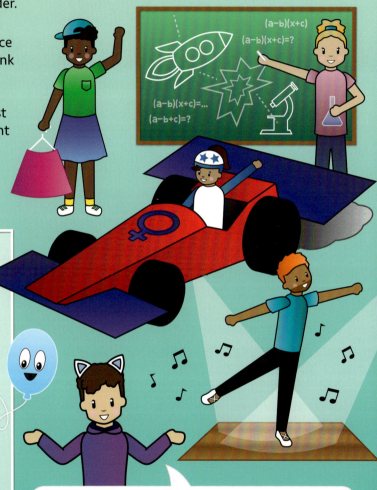

**Try this:** Answer these questions or discuss them with your class or a friend.

**1.** Do you think you could guess everything about a person from just their gender? Would it be a fair guess?

**2.** Do you think there are some toys, clothes or hobbies that are associated with a particular gender?

**3.** Is there pressure on some people to hide their emotions because of their gender?

**4.** What advice would you give to someone about being themselves, whatever their gender is?

'Our gender shouldn't decide our likes/dislikes, style, emotions, ambitions or futures. We should be and do whatever feels right for us, regardless of gender.'

# Romantic Love

There are many different types of love: how about the love you have for your family? Or the love you might have for your pet? What about the love you have for your favourite food or even your favourite song? Can you think of any other types of love?

Romantic love is a type of love which people might feel for each other. It can happen at different times for different people.

You may have seen ideas of romantic love in films or storybooks. What do you think about it? Do you think it looks a bit silly? Or does it look appealing? Sometimes, in stories, people will do daring things for love like fight a dragon, or climb a tower or travel across the world.

Now those ideas are all pretty extreme! But what these stories are trying to explain to us is that romantic love can be incredibly powerful and it can make us experience some very strong emotions.

A person who is experiencing love for the first time might start to have all sorts of new and different feelings. They may feel butterflies in their tummy or they may be unable to concentrate. It can all be very exciting but it will also be different for everybody.

Sometimes the beginning of this type of love is called 'falling in love' and it usually starts with something called 'attraction'.

Two people who are experiencing attraction may want to spend time together, to get to know each other. They might want to share experiences as a way of building their relationship and growing their love.

They may also want to express their attraction or love for each other with their bodies. They might hold hands, hug or even kiss. It is very important that both people are happy to do this and they should clearly ask their partner whether it is OK or not.

Some romantic couples may wish to get married and others might not, some couples might wish to have children and some might not, some couples might stay together forever and some might not. It's about finding what is right for you.

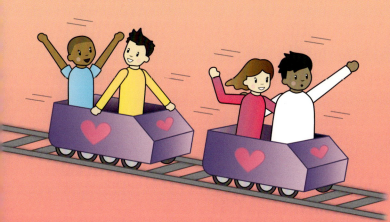

Romantic love can be a bit of a roller coaster. It may at times be fun, cute, silly, happy and easy.
At other times it might be difficult, sad and even disappointing. It will be different things at different times for everyone.

A lot of romantic love is about feelings and it helps if couples can explain to each other how they are feeling, even if it's not always the easiest thing to do.

## Aromantic

Some people do not experience romantic love and that's fine, too. A person who experiences little or no romantic attraction towards others may call themselves aromantic.

# Sexual Orientation

People can be attracted to each other for a number of reasons. One reason might be because of another person's gender or sex. This is called sexual orientation.

When it comes to sexual orientation not everyone feels the same. In fact, there are a number of different orientations that exist, and below are some very basic explanations of just some of them.

### Heterosexual

This is when a man is attracted to a woman and when a woman is attracted to a man.

This is sometimes also known as 'straight'.

### Gay

Gay is a word used to describe men who are attracted to other men and women who are attracted to other women.

### Lesbian

Lesbian is another word used to describe women who are attracted to other women.

### Bisexual

Someone who is bisexual is attracted to more than one gender.

(Although not necessarily at the same time or the same amount.)

## Pansexual

For someone who is pansexual, gender may not be important. They could be attracted to someone of any gender.

## Asexual

Some people will feel little or no sexual attraction for other people at all. This is called being asexual.

(Someone who is asexual may still develop and enjoy a romantic relationship with another person.)

Some people will happily use these words to describe their sexual orientation, whilst some people will use other labels and some people may prefer not being labelled at all.

Some people will see sexual orientation as a spectrum (like gender) where a person can sit, float, or move between different orientations.

The most important things to remember are that sexual orientation is personal, that everyone will experience it in their own way, and that all sexual orientations and relationships are equally valid.

'Your own sexual orientation isn't something you need to know or think about right now. It will likely be something that you discover as you grow older and it is something that will happen naturally, when the time is right for you.'

**Try This:** Cut out the 'Mix and Match Worksheet' on page 33. See if you can match up the orientations with the correct definitions.

# Privilege

Privilege is when life is a bit easier for someone, just because of their identity (who they are).

A running race wouldn't be fair if everyone started from a different place, would it?

In life we all start from different places because we all have different identities.

Unfortunately our world favours some identities more than others, often because those are the identities who have been in charge.

Imagine a world of shapes where triangles are in charge. All the doors are triangle-shaped, along with the beds, chairs and clothes. Everything in this world works for triangles really well, so well that triangles don't even notice how easy life is for them and how hard life is for other shapes.

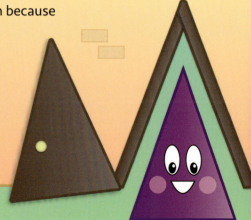

In this world, the other shapes have to work harder to fit in. In this world, triangles have lots of privilege but the other shapes do not.

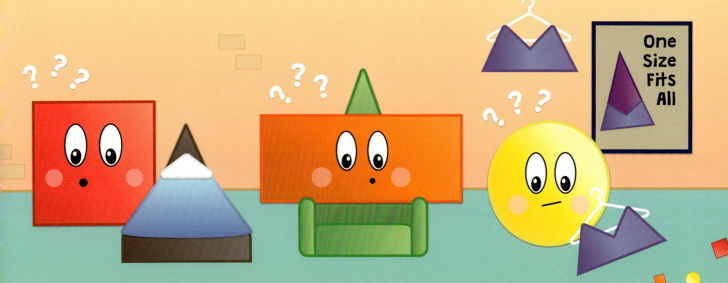

Our world can sometimes be a bit like this and, like the triangles, sometimes we just don't notice the things which make life easy for us and harder for other people.

### Things That Can Affect a Person's Privilege:

- Race, Colour
- Nationality
- Ability/Disability
- Gender
- Sexual Orientation
- Culture
- Religion
- Education
- Body Size

'Remember, whilst a person can be privileged in some ways, they may not be in others.'

**Try this:** Answer these questions or discuss them with your class or a friend.

1. How might different identities be affected by privilege?

2. What might they experience?

3. What else might affect a person's privilege?

4. In an ideal world, life wouldn't be easier or harder for anyone. Do you think that this is possible?

# Discrimination

Discrimination is the unfair treatment of one person, or a group of people, because of their identity. This could be...

- A shop refusing to serve a customer because of their sexual orientation.
- A company paying a person less because of their gender.
- Using hateful language towards a person because of their religion.

Discrimination is a bit like bullying. It means people get left out and treated badly, simply because of who they are (their identity). It is unfair and can leave a lasting, negative impact on a person.

## What Does the Law Say?

In the UK we have a law called 'The Equality Act 2010'. This law is here to protect people from being treated unequally and it makes discrimination illegal.

'The Equality Act 2010' states that the following characteristics are protected...

Age · Race · Religion or Belief

Disability · Sex · Sexual Orientation

**Marriage and Civil Partnership**  **Pregnancy and Maternity**  **Gender Reassignment**

This law applies at school, work, at the doctor's, in a shop or anywhere you go. It is everyone's job to make sure people are treated equally and fairly. It is the job of the police and the courts to enforce this law.

Equality and fairness are important values in our country and that is why we have this law in the UK. Other countries across the world have similar laws; however this is not the case everywhere.

Sadly, there are still some countries where laws exist that discriminate against people's identities and this can make life very difficult for many people.

## What do you think?

**1.** What do you think about this law?

**2.** Has anyone been left out?

**3.** Do you think the language of this law could be more inclusive?

**4.** How would you feel if you were treated unfairly just for being you?

**5.** What can be done to help people in the UK and other countries facing discrimination?

# The First Pride

The word Pride means to feel good about who you are. Every year around the world Pride events are opportunities for LGBT+ people (and their allies) to celebrate their identities (and each other's) whilst standing up for equal rights.

But where do these Pride events come from? Well, let's go back to 1969, New York City, and a bar called The Stonewall Inn.

The Stonewall Inn was one of the few places in New York where LGBT+ people could go to be themselves, because sadly at this time in history, LGBT+ people were not treated fairly - in fact they were treated very badly.

LGBT+ people were often fired from their jobs, disowned by their families, and some were even arrested, simply because of who they were and who they loved.

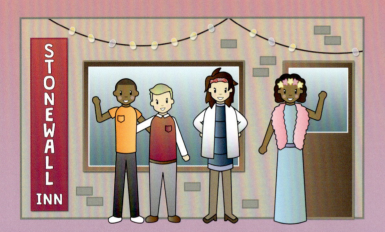

But at The Stonewall Inn, LGBT+ people were safe to be who they were... Or so they thought...

On the evening of June 28th 1969, the New York police decided to raid The Stonewall Inn and planned to arrest the LGBT+ people inside. Raids on bars like The Stonewall Inn had become common and it was something many LGBT+ people had grown used to... However, on this particular night, at this particular bar, something was different.

No one knows exactly what sparked it, but the LGBT+ people inside had all grown tired of their unfair treatment and together they decided 'ENOUGH!'

LGBT+ people knew they deserved equality, respect and freedom... so they protested and refused to be arrested. It was quite a dangerous thing to do, but still, they stood strongly together for what they believed in.

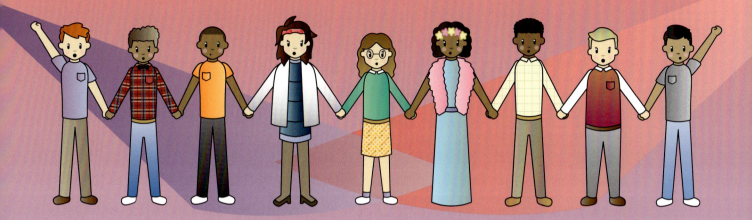

The police eventually backed down and this night became an important step towards LGBT+ equality.

Exactly one year later, a parade was organised in New York to remember the events of The Stonewall Inn and how the LGBT+ community stood up to inequality. Each year, this parade grew and grew and it has now become what we know today as Pride.

Pride is a day to celebrate freedom and equality for the LGBT+ community, a day to remember those who stood up for justice and a day to be proud, whoever you are.

The first UK Pride was held in London on July 1st 1972. Now Pride events are held in towns and cities across the UK and around the world.

'If something is unfair or wrong, we can stand up for what we believe is right and help influence change. We are all equal and deserve to be treated fairly.'

**Try this:** Answer these questions or discuss them with your class or a friend.

**1.** Do you think it's OK to break the law when it discriminates against people?

**2.** Can you think of any other examples of when people have stood up against unfairness?

**3.** Can you think of any groups of people who are still treated unfairly today?

**4.** What can we do to help them?

# How Can I Help?

If you've noticed that life can be a bit tougher for some people because of their identity, maybe you'd like to help. This is called being an 'ally'.

Being an ally means you support fair and equal treatment for others regardless of their identity. Allies take action to make the world fairer.

Below are some things that allies do. Can you think of any more ideas?

Wear or Display their Support

Write to their MP

Stand Up for Others

March or Peacefully Protest

# So, What Does LGBT+ Mean?

Well, if you've made it this far then you already know! LGBT+ stands for...

## Lesbian  Gay  Bisexual
## Transgender

 The + is used to represent other identities such as Non-Binary, Intersex, Pansexual, Asexual, Aromantic and more. The + sign is a good way of including as many identities as possible.

**LGBT+** basically represents a community of people who identify as anything other then straight or cisgender.

Sometimes you might see the letters **LGBTQ+**. Here the letter **Q** can stand for 'Questioning' which means a person who is questioning (or exploring) their identity. It can also stand for 'Queer' which can mean someone who feels they are not totally straight or not totally cisgender.

Some people will identify as more than one letter and that is OK, too.

Some of the identities in this book are similar and some are different, but they are all often grouped together under the title LGBT+ because, throughout history, these identities have all experienced similar challenges. They've often had to face the same types of discrimination and have all been treated unfairly.

'Remember, all these words are fine to use (they're not bad words), but just be sure to use them respectfully, with care and never as an insult.'

'LGBT+ equality has come a long way, thanks to some incredible groups and individuals. By learning what LGBT+ means you are helping to make the world more fair and equal.'

# LGBT+ People

LGBT+ people have always existed and can be found everywhere. They are different ages, races, religions, abilities, nationalities and cultures. They have different jobs, different thoughts and different experiences.

Like all the identities mentioned in this book, an LGBT+ identity is simply just one way of being human.

# LGBT+ Flag Guide

Here are just some of the different LGBT+ flags that currently exist. You might see these at Pride celebrations, on various buildings and even being worn. Displaying these flags is a great way of letting LGBT+ people know that they are welcome.

# Need to Talk?

We hope you enjoyed this book and that it was helpful. As we said at the start, you may now have more questions or would like a bit more information about certain topics. If you do then perhaps you can talk to an adult who you trust, like a parent, guardian or teacher.

However, if you feel that you are not able to talk to anyone around you, then don't panic because there are other options. Below are two UK-based helplines that you can call if you want to talk to someone about **anything.**

These helplines are free, confidential and they are here to support young people.

## Childline
childline.org.uk

### 0800 1111

A free, private service for children where you can talk about anything.

## Mermaids
mermaidsuk.org.uk

### 0808 801 0400

A UK charity who support transgender, non-binary and gender-diverse children, young people, and their families.

'Don't EVER feel like you are alone, because you are not. There will always be someone to listen.'

# Identity

### Use, copy or photocopy this worksheet.
### (A downloadable version is available at popnolly.com/free-resources)

Our identity is not just one thing, in fact it is made up of lots of different things. What makes up your identity?

Fill in the boxes. Maybe you can share your answers with a friend?

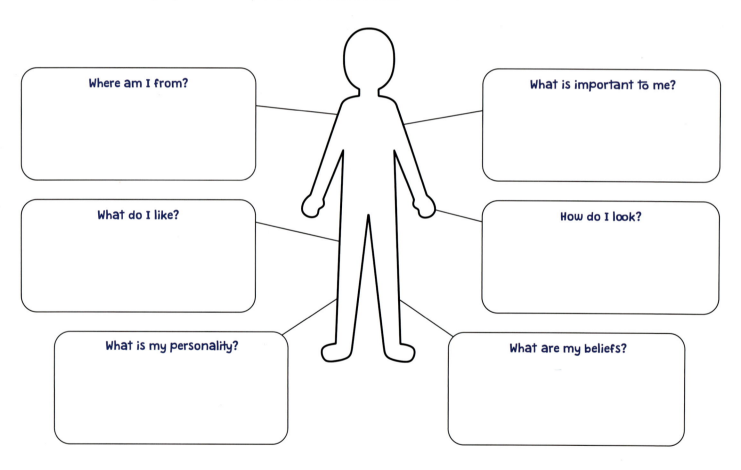

**Name:** ..............................................

### Heterosexual

When a man is attracted to a woman and when a woman is attracted to a man.

### Gay

A word used to describe men who are attracted to other men and women who are attracted to other women.

### Lesbian

Another word used to describe women who are attracted to other women.

### Bisexual

A person who is attracted to more than one gender.

### Pansexual

Gender may not be important to this person. They could be attracted to someone of any gender.

### Asexual

A person who experiences little or no sexual attraction to others.

# Pop'n'Olly

### Creating a More Accepting Society for Future Generations

Pop'n'Olly is an LGBT+ and equality focused educational resource used by children, parents, carers and teachers. Our videos and books are used in primary schools across the UK, and beyond, to teach about equality, diversity and acceptance.

Our fun, informative and colourful content is inclusive of diverse characters and ultimately aims to combat LGBT+ prejudice before it can even begin to form.

Our mission is to create a more accepting society for future generations whilst inspiring children to act whenever they see someone else's human rights being compromised.

Discover our content and resources at popnolly.com.

# Olly Pike

Olly Pike is the creator of Pop'n'Olly Ltd. He writes the stories, draws the pictures, animates the videos and even stars in them! Using skills learnt from his theatrical, and children's television, background, Olly creates inclusive content that is fun and informative.

Olly is a regular LGBT+ education panellist and media guest and his work has been highly praised and shared amongst the LGBT+ and inclusive education community. Countless schools, charities, organisations and companies regularly use Olly's content as part of their LGBT+ inclusive practice.

Having been shortlisted for a 'National Diversity' and a 'Gay Times Honours' award, Olly has also spoken in Parliament and London City Hall and has showcased his work at events such as 'The Children's Media Conference', 'Stonewall's Education For All Conference' and 'The NEU LGBT+ Educators Conference'. In 2020 Olly made the UK's Pride Power List and in 2021 Olly was awarded an *Attitude Pride Award*.

Olly has also created content for *CBeebies*, *Tate Kids* and *Hopster TV*, and collaborated with UK charities *Stonewall* and *Mermaids*. To date, Olly has distributed over 15,000 copies of his LGBT+ and equality-inclusive books to children, parents and teachers around the world, and the Pop'n'Olly YouTube channel continues to receive millions of views.

# Mel Lane & James Canning

Mel has worked for many years as a primary school teacher and teacher trainer. James is a university student passionate about maths and physics.

This mother and son team work together with Dorset's LGBT+ youth charity, *Space Youth Project*, to deliver staff training and workshops in schools for students aged 4 to 18.

They passionately believe that all young people deserve to learn about LGBT+ identities to enable everyone to be true to themselves.

Find out more about Mel's work at diversitymel.com and on Instagram @diversity_mel.

# More Classroom Resources

Get access to our entire classroom resource library (and more) when you become a Pop'n'Olly member at popnolly.com/membership.

Our classroom resources have been created with the help of teachers and educators, and are designed to be used alongside our books and free videos.

Easy to use as part of English, Maths, History, Art, Drama and PSHE lessons, these diverse and inclusive resources explore problem-solving, storytelling, discovery, creativity, understanding, empathy, kindness and acceptance.

## Printable Worksheets, Lesson Plans & Videos

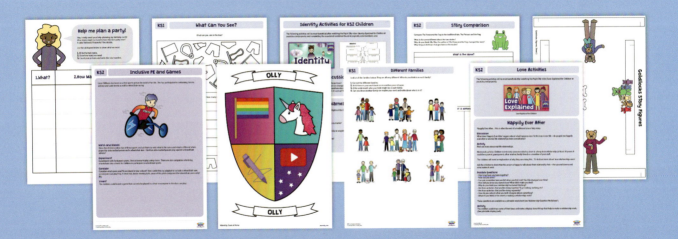

## Printable Classroom Posters

# More Books

## popnolly.com/shop

Pop'n'Olly's inclusive children's picture books are used across the UK, and beyond, in classrooms and homes. Our adapted fairy tales and stories introduce diverse characters to children in a familiar way whilst promoting understanding and acceptance.

While the reading levels of our books may vary, all of our stories can be enjoyed by any age. Our books can be used as part of school lessons or to open up discussion at home.

Available from popnolly.com/shop, *Amazon* or ask at your local bookshop.

ISBN 9780993340741

### 'Prince Henry' – An Equality Fairy Tale

Join Henry in his fairy tale kingdom where certain laws apply when it comes to choosing who you can spend your life with. A gay fairy tale romance for young readers, where class is the discriminating factor rather than sexuality. *Prince Henry* delivers a positive message of both love and equality. (Key Stage 1 & 2.)

ISBN 9780993340734

### 'Jamie' – A Transgender Cinderella Story

What happens when you don't have a fairy godmother to grant your every wish? Jamie doesn't. So she finds her own way to go to the ball. A story of determination, hard work and transition. With some clever mice and a pumpkin car, join Jamie as she becomes... Jamie. (Key Stage 2.)

ISBN 9780993340758

### 'Princess Penny & the Pea' – An Inclusive Fairy Tale

It's not easy being a princess. There are so many rules. Penny just wants to have fun like everyone else. Find out what happens when an unexpected dinner guest leads to a number of zany trials and challenges. A tale that questions whether our differences should determine how we are treated. (Key Stage 1 & 2.)

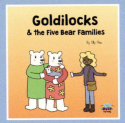

ISBN 9780993340741

### 'Goldilocks & the Five Bear Families' – Family Diversity

An adapted fairy tale designed to teach early readers about family diversity. Join Goldilocks as she ventures into the village to meet a diverse mix of different bear families. (Key Stage 1.)

ISBN 9781785923821

### 'The Prince and the Frog' – Healthy Relationships

A story which teaches children about same-sex relationships and attraction. Exploring what it means to be in a healthy, loving relationship, *The Prince and the Frog* encourages children to listen to others, be kind, and embrace diversity and equality. Includes a lesson plan. (Key Stage 1 & 2.)

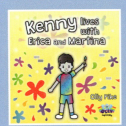

ISBN 9780993340772

### 'Kenny lives with Erica and Martina'

*Kenny lives with Erica and Martina* is an original story inspired by the 1981 book 'Jenny lives with Eric and Martin' by the Danish author Susanne Bösche.

Our book tells the story of Kenny whose grey world soon becomes a lot more colourful with the arrival of some new neighbours.

Kenny and his mums welcome the change, but this can't be said for everyone who lives on Kenny's street. Kenny has to somehow let everyone know that being different is not something to be afraid of.

*Kenny lives with Erica and Martina* aims to teach children about diversity, equality and acceptance. (Key Stage 1 & 2.)

Our aim is to get a copy of this book into every UK Primary School.

Help us achieve this by visiting www.lgbteducation.co.uk.

# Thank You

Thank you to all those who follow, champion and support Pop'n'Olly. A big thank you to all the teachers, parents, children and LGBT+ experts who assisted with the creation of this book and a very special thank you to the people below. - *Olly, Mel and James*